1 The first spacewalk

On 18 March 1965, Alexei Leonov blasted off in his ship, *Voskhod 2*. His mission, to become the first human to walk in space, nearly ended in disaster.

the first spacewalk

Alexei Leonov

In orbit around Earth, he climbed into his spacecraft's inflatable **airlock**, *Volga*, which was attached to the side of his ship.

The air drained away, then Leonov opened the outer hatch and floated into the **vacuum** of space. He was attached to the ship only by a five-metre-long **tether**.

He **marvelled** at the silence. The only sounds were his own breathing and the beating of his heart.

He marvelled at Earth below him.

He marvelled at the **cosmos**, stretching out around him.

"I was surrounded by stars … floating without much control."

After 12 minutes, it was time to come back inside, but there was a problem. His spacesuit had begun to **inflate**. Soon, his hands slipped out of his gloves, and his feet slipped out of his boots.

The more he struggled to get back to the airlock, the more he sweated. He felt like he was sloshing in sweat. When he finally got there, he could no longer fit inside. His suit was rigid. He was in desperate trouble.

His only chance was to **depressurise** the suit. Somehow, Leonov managed to open a **valve**, which let some air out.

However, this meant he began to suffer decompression sickness (known as "the bends").

Luckily, Leonov was able to **deflate** his suit just enough to haul himself back inside the airlock and close the hatch.

After **jettisoning** the inflatable airlock, *Voskhod 2* returned to Earth with its exhausted astronaut.

2 The first Moon landing

On 20 July 1969, around 650 million people across the world gathered around their TVs and radios to witness the first Moon landing.

Apollo 11's cramped lunar **module**, *Eagle*, was crewed by Neil Armstrong and Buzz Aldrin.

Apollo 11 crew checking out the command module

In orbit above the Moon, they undocked from their command module, *Columbia*.

Aldrin fired the ignition, and the engine roared to life, carrying them down towards the surface.

They were heading for an area called the Sea of Tranquillity.

the *Eagle* module coming in to land on the Moon

Moments later, an alarm code flashed up on their display: "12-02".

Neither man knew what this code meant, but any alarm was serious and could ruin the mission.

Armstrong radioed Mission Control back on Earth. "Program alarm, code 1202."

There was a tense moment while everyone waited.

Fortunately, one of the Mission Control experts knew the answer. The code meant the computer simply had too much to do. But it was OK, because it would just restart and keep going.

"We're GO on that alarm!"

The astronauts breathed a sigh of relief and continued their descent.

With only a few hundred metres to go, Armstrong noticed that the computer was guiding them towards a large boulder-filled crater. It was too rocky to land there.

Armstrong took the controls, steering them over the crater in search of a better landing spot.

Then, another warning flashed up. They were running out of fuel!

Looking down at the bright grey surface, they saw the **silhouette** of their moon lander. It looked like a spider, bristling with **antennae** and landing gear.

With just seconds of fuel remaining, *Eagle* settled gently on the Moon and the engine stopped.

"Houston. Tranquillity Base here. The Eagle has landed."

The whole world breathed a sigh of relief.

A few hours later, Armstrong and Aldrin took the first human steps on the lunar surface.

"That's one small step for man, one giant leap for mankind."

3 Explorers on the Moon

On 30 July 1971, *Apollo 15* astronauts, Dave Scott and Jim Irwin, coasted over the crests of the Moon's Apennine Mountains, landing their lunar module, *Falcon*, nearby.

"OK, Houston, the Falcon is on the plain at Hadley."

As Scott hopped down the ladder, he eyed Mount Hadley Delta, which towered 3,353 metres above. Its steep slopes would be their target. But how would they get there?

The answer was folded up on the side of the *Falcon*: the Lunar Roving Vehicle (LRV). Once assembled, it would help them get across the lunar surface.

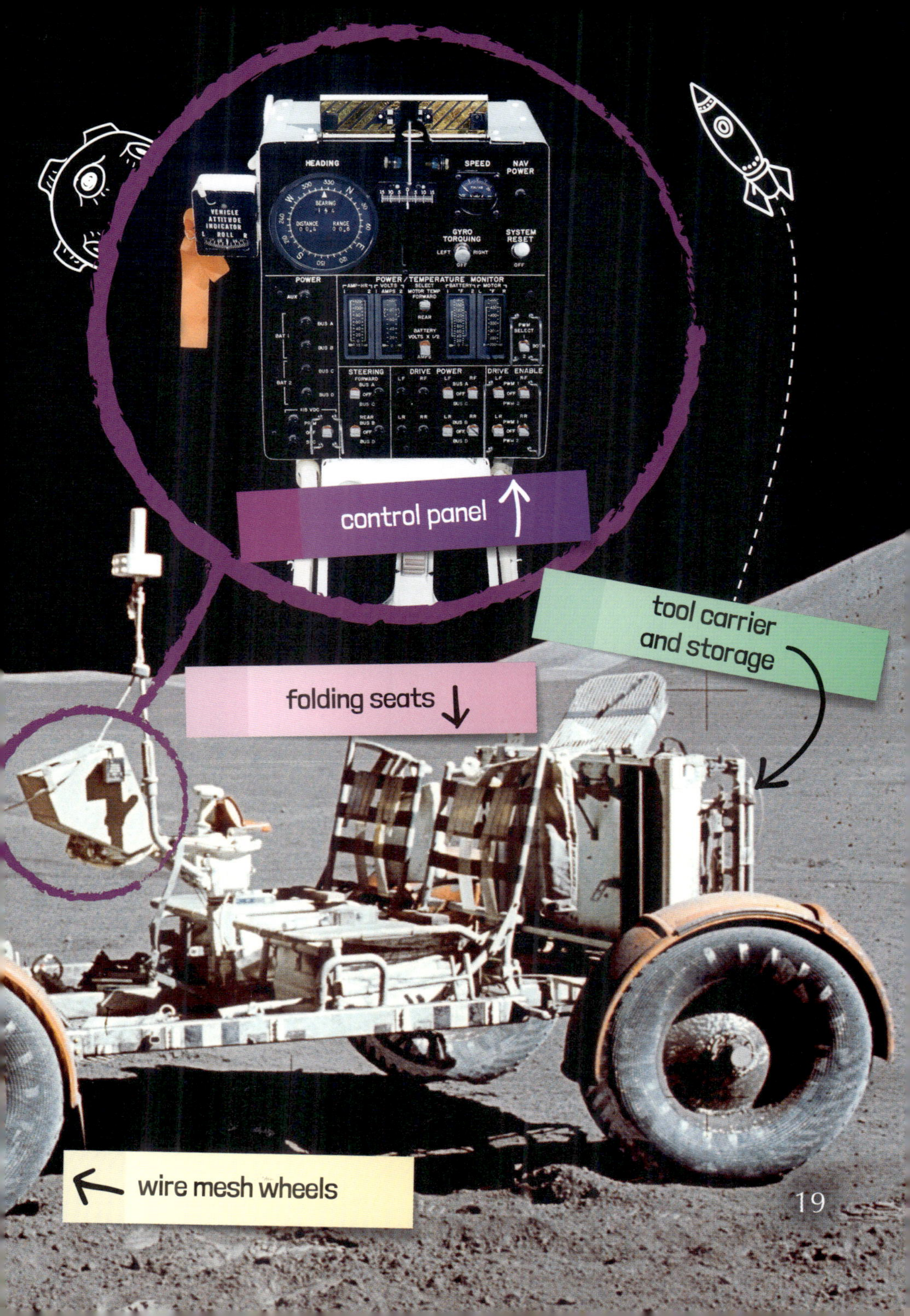
HEADING
SPEED
NAV POWER
GYRO TORQUING
SYSTEM RESET
POWER
POWER/TEMPERATURE MONITOR
STEERING
DRIVE POWER
DRIVE ENABLE
control panel
tool carrier and storage
folding seats
wire mesh wheels

The two men set off on their rover. It was hard driving. They had to steer round huge craters and boulders the size of houses. In the Moon's low gravity, every time the rover hit a bump, it nearly took off!

an artist's impression of driving on the Moon

an astronaut loading rock samples

The mountain peaks glinted gold in the sunlight. Below them, a spectacular canyon called Hadley Rille wound off into the distance. And above them, blue Earth shone bright in the dark of space.

Later, on the slopes of the mountain, they spotted a small, white rock. Scott lifted it carefully with his tongs. A layer of ancient dust fell away, to reveal sparkling crystals.

"Guess what we just found?"

They knew by the sparkles that they'd found something very special.

When they eventually returned to Earth, tests showed the rock was four and a half billion years old and was a piece of the Moon's early crust. It became known as the *Genesis Rock*.

the Genesis Rock

After a three-day mission, Scott drove their trusty rover to its final resting spot a hundred metres away. From there, it filmed *Falcon* lifting off.

4 Rendezvous in space

On a farm in Iowa, USA, in 1969, nine-year-old Peggy Whitson watched TV as Neil Armstrong and Buzz Aldrin touched down on the Moon.

"Cool job!" she thought, swiftly deciding that she too wanted to be an astronaut someday.

NASA began accepting female astronauts in 1977. But when Peggy applied for astronaut training, she was turned down again and again. It took ten years before NASA finally accepted her.

Peggy Whitson, Astronaut Candidate Class of 1996

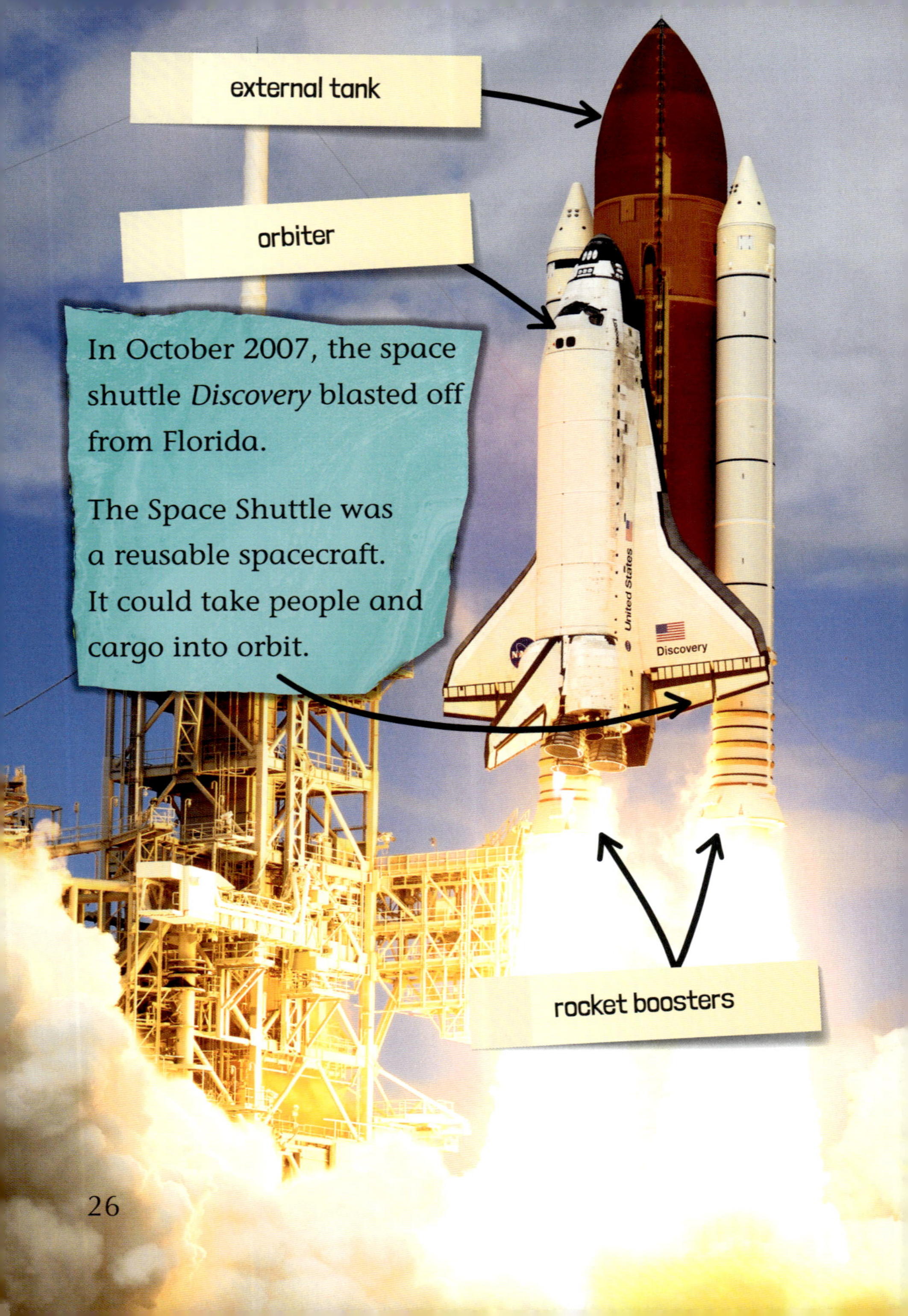

In October 2007, the space shuttle *Discovery* blasted off from Florida.

The Space Shuttle was a reusable spacecraft. It could take people and cargo into orbit.

The shuttle's commander was Pamela A Melroy, an ex-airforce test pilot. Once in orbit, Commander Melroy docked with the International Space Station (ISS). The hatch opened, she reached through and shook hands with the commander of the ISS, who was none other than …

Peggy Whitson.

It was the first meeting of two female commanders in space, and a key moment for female astronauts.

Glossary

airlock an airtight chamber which lets an astronaut go out into space without losing the breathable air inside their spacecraft

antennae devices that send and receive radio waves

cosmos the universe

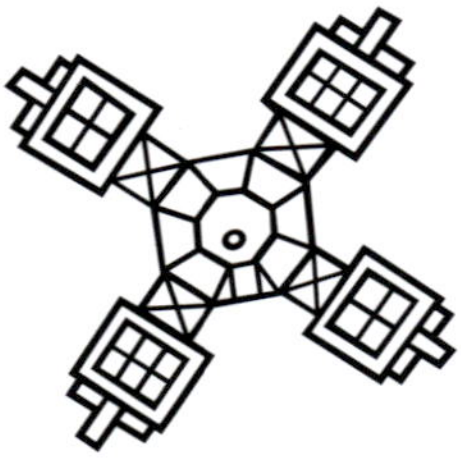

deflate to let air out of

depressurise to lower the amount of air

inflate to blow up

jettisoning leaving behind

marvelled looked with surprise and wonder

module part of a spaceship that can break away and carry out its own special tasks

silhouette a shadow

tether a cable that stops an astronaut floating off into space

vacuum a place with no air

valve a device that lets something in or out, for example, air

Index

Can you save the day?

What should the astronauts do next?

Alexei Leonov: "My spacesuit has inflated. I can't get back inside the ship!"

Neil Armstrong: "The computer is guiding the lunar module towards a big crater!"

Dave Scott:
"Landing went without a hitch. But how do we get to Mount Hadley Delta?"

Peggy Whitson:
"NASA keeps rejecting me for astronaut training. Should I give up on my dream?"

Ideas for reading

Written by Gill Matthews
Primary Literacy Consultant

Reading objectives:

- be introduced to non-fiction books that are structured in different ways
- draw on what they already know or on background information and vocabulary provided by the teacher
- check that the text makes sense to them as they read and correcting inaccurate reading
- answer and ask questions

Spoken language objectives:

- ask relevant questions to extend their understanding and knowledge
- use relevant strategies to build their vocabulary
- articulate and justify answers, arguments and opinions

Curriculum links: History: events beyond living memory that are significant nationally or globally

Word count: 1287

Interest words: dramatic, disaster, struggled, desperate, haul

Build a context for reading

- Ask children to look at the front cover and to read the title. Explore what they know about space and space travel.
- Read the back-cover blurb. Check whether children are unfamiliar with any of the vocabulary in the blurb and support them in working out the meanings.
- Ask why the children think a Moon landing might be nerve-wracking and a spacewalk might be near-fatal.
- Ask children to find the contents page. Discuss the purpose and organisation of a contents. Children can use the contents to find the chapter called *The first spacewalk*.

BIG Moments in Space

Contents

Written by David Macphail

Collins

Space is an exciting place! And dangerous, too!

Since Yuri Gagarin's first spaceflight in 1961, there have been many big dramatic moments.

Yuri Gagarin